BLOOMING
RSES

BLOOMING ROSES

SUMIRASKO

PARTRIDGE

A Penguin Company

Partridge books may be ordered through booksellers or by contacting:

Partridge India
Penguin Books India Pvt.Ltd
11, Community Centre, Panchsheel Park, New Delhi 110017
India
www.partridgepublishing.com
Phone: 000.800.10062.62

Contents

1. Creative Fever 1
2. Divine Love 3
3. Motion 4
4. Squares 5
5. I remember 7
6. The Mist 8
7. She is fancy of delight.. 9
8. In Distress 10
9. Love's Dream 11
10. The Silence 12
11. Destiny... 13
12. No Panacea (Godesia).. 15
13. 'Lean on me' 16
14. Diseased thoughts... 17
15. Express... 18
16. The Snare 19
17. In the arms of emotion 20
18. When the bus ran away (1983–86) 21
19. Distant horizens come nigh.. 23
20. The Square.. 24
21. The anabolic ambit 25
22. Insecurity 27
23. The Feminine Principle 29
24. Perfect Indecision 30
25. My Monalisa... 31
26. City to Village and Sacrilege 32
27. Vision.. 33
28. On Peace.. 34
29. The Diary 35
30. Recollected Ecstasy... 37
31. Love is Salvation... 38
32. January... 39
33. Conquest.. 40
34. Interrogated 41
35. The Man... 43
36. Borrowed thoughts 44

37.   Unnatural Love..46
38.   Unmarked Harte..47
39.   On Morality and Mortality...................................48
40.   Perfume...50
41.   Complete Dependence 51
42.   Living Lucy 52
43.   The Feminine Principle 53
44.   Awake 54
45.   On Personal Liberty..56
46.   Life and Death...58
47.   The Drunkard..60
48.   Destiny..62
49.   Cold Fusion 63
50.   Rupturns Mirth 64
51.   Spiritual Leisure 65
52.   Joyful Hate...66
53.   The Liar...67
54.   Sandwitched 68
55.   Round the clock...69
56.   Just Vainful..70
57.   The Man..72
58.   OHIO..74
59.   Goddess of Love 75
60.   Effort 76
61.   Too Deep 78
62.   Intermission 80
63.   My Verses 82
64.   Truly far 83
65.   Come on 84
66.   Unseen Love 85
67.   Tired...86
68.   Little or No..87
69.   In a dark room 89
70.   Vices Eternized..90
71.   Come into me 'O God' 91
72.   I must have been like 92
73.   The Blank Paper...93
74.   Death—The Brute..94
75.   She was a fair Sight..95
76.   When Love Calls..96
77.   Dracula 97

78. Wind of Remembrance...99
79. Celestis...100
80. My Moon...101
81. There was no beauty 102
82. Confession 103
83. The Mystery Joyful..104
84. Only human..105
85. The Stare 106
86. Real Roses..108
87. On College 109
88. The Magic Morphia 111
89. The Wounded Man 113
90. Lost in the wild...114
91. More than Mother...115
92. In a Saloon...117
93. La Dien de La Danse 119
94. Always Near...122
95. Back and fill Life 123
96. Just Now 124
97. On Critics..125
98. In the Present Sky...126
99. The Secret Lover 127
100. The Mud 128
101. At Dawn 129
102. Now its my Turn 130
103. 'Greater than Life'..132
104. The Questioner (Weathered) Leaf 133
105. Levin...134
106. India...135
107. An Insane Walk 137
108. An elegy for doomed youth 139

Blooming Roses is a collection of 108 poems selected by me. Poet himself says his creative verses are like blood flowing in his veins. Ideas of poet and his philosphy will be appreciated by the thinkers and citizens including young youths of college and schools alike.

His poems have attracted the attcution of the entire world. So we request only to read and have across to Sumirasko's wonderful world of creations. Your feedback to me and publishers will encourage us.

Er. Vivekanand Pd.
Retd. Director (S.E.) WRD,
Bihar Govt. Patna—800001

Creative Fever

More beward 'mylove' lean on some one safe
      break this ligament, I will live
   but a voice strong dictates from deep
     thou I will break your life's string
          you 'many death' 'mylove'
     Says another from surface
Like a cool lamb, I will be content, happy
      happy in your happiness
   but the man that is me
      cries savagely for possessiveness
You are human, free to make a choice
        lacks that up this in human voice
  a self in machoism wants laceration
     the other demands a sadistic rejoice
The greatest sacrifice, the greatest vice
      go together
    quarreling, competing, tormenting
      wind against wind
        storm against storm
      gale against gale
   crossed I am, pierced with nails
      gripped with fever, strange fever
  helpless, I make no choice
      only express honestly the two
  express care and hostility
      See! it is poetry
   Sublimity and crude revenge
      go together
this fever which has eloped with faith
     is creative
        is a creative fever

II

No. more fear my 'love'
the hawk is no more, no more is the dove
a new creature, only ore
has been born on Earth
in this moment the ecstasy is mine
I feel myself as divine
the fever will return, I will shiver again
feel the eternal, eternal pain
give it a creative, a creative name

Sumirasko
146 Dt. 02.09.1993, 8.45 A.M.

Divine Love

The storm takes a leaf green up
flying higher and higher
Soaring higher and above the clouds
      the clouds sauntering
  I am rising, rising in love with you
There is a gale, blowing in my harte
you sit on the marble throne
      I cry 'hail'
  hour after hour, day after day
      you rule me 'o fay'
  your face when I behold
      a garden of flowers I see
    that depends not on season
      your face always a beatific vision
    my love betrays my reason
overwhelm me your eyes deep
      Waves rolling in them I see
in love's ocean I drown to rise
      rise take a divine leap
  your divine love
      flying over and above

Sumirasko
147 Dt. 02.09.1993, 10.30 A.M.

Motion

On wycliff's high hill
  the silly air plays the tune
there is a fall
  that falls from height
there are rare weeds that delight
  near, mistresses clamour for motion
  to catch the falling star at night
Their nose always backing up
  their mouth always fed
Water quenches their physical thirst
   ephimera stars are
    in plenty, plenty for lust
Such is the scene on wycliff's hill
  their life motion
like the waterfall
   while thoughts sleep
move not deep
  for they, all eat the mandrake weed
They say near wycliff's high hill
   there is emotion
for, they have send thousand men
   not one came back
So all found devotion
But I have seen dusty bones
  flowing in life's stream
too gruesome a death to dream
  convinced I am
   near wycliff's hill
motion is serene
  Life is an indifferent dream
mistresses are content and mean
   Where then go too keen

Sumirasko
149 Dt. 02.09.1993, 04.30 P.M.

Squares

Absent mindedly walk
        aimless tread
When mystery deepens
        legs find themselves
      where directions meet
        meet and separate
      the place becomes a square
        condition desperate
Infinite regress . . . Infinite progress
        both await
Infinite hate . . . . Infinite love
        waits fate
     on the square where
        Life crosses death
     are both garlands and wreath
you think . . . . you reason
        reason to perfection
you question . . . . you answer
        find . . . answering is no solution
in harte you decide
        unable to live in indecision
you waited not enough
        too costly is this cowardice
your life was on the square
        in the first crisis
you felt it not there
        and now you are in deep slumber
you see the world

Again if the axe falls—you better scream
better close your eyes . . . investigate
        if a square is seen
gruesome in pain on no one lean
        endure, let decision arise from within
like you feel life, feel the wind
                        warm or cool
                intensity, feel the cup brimming
from squares life begins

Sumirasko
148 Dt. 02.09.1993, 02.55 P.M.

I remember

I remember my life's history
     my actions which were a mystery
tread that moved all around
     and found soothing ground
I remember the freezing warm breeze
       equivocations that were life's lease
remember the laughing sky
     remember the strange tie
that binded me to misery
     Remember moving love's high tide
that drowned me savagely
     Sarcastic faces, doubting eyes
that behaved most wickedly
     remember hour long didactic jargons
how to mend my mind insanely
      yet condemned to repeat I am
       repeating that, remembered, history

Sumirasko
150 Dt. 02.90.1993, 5.45 A.M.

The Mist

on wintry dawn
        upon Earth's face
on flowers on roads, on thorns
        upon the glassy window
small drops hang
        small drops haze the morn
So coolly nature sweats
        after a night long foil
on every track that hug across
        hazy distances eye gave
their is a doubtful turmoil

II

My eyes see too the same mist
        in the same mist you looks strange
you are not anywhere here
        but eyes see you change
Alibi is the mist for you
        my own mist of doubts
and though your fragrance is sweet
        my thoughts clamour love
In the mist all is unclear
        unclear your face my love
this dawn can only hear not see
        the fluttering wings of a dove

III

I wait for a clue for my love
        wait for the saviour
wait for the sun that will arise from East
        arise from within to clear the mist

Sumirasko
151 Dt. 02.09.1993, 5.55 P.M.

She is fancy of delight

She is a fancy of delight
    a fair lovely starry night
lovely full moon is her face
    million stars shine in her grace
darkness in between potrays her shame
    like a delightful fancy in life she came
      has no other name
A fancy as real as the moon that shines
    if it is lost for nights
Will you call it a dream?
    her face disappears for days from sight
but her star like grace always rains
    rains on me from above
She comes not nigh for too profound
      is her same
    She is fancy of rare delight
    yet she has a real name

Sumirasko
152 Dt. 03.09.1993, 7.30 A.M.

In Distress

These satrical parents
    they will know never my worth
like the flower that knows
    not its own sap
Which is an elixir for the bee
Even a flower is more intelligent
    protects the sap is forever vigilant
but these dead humen
    kill the sap with insect repellents
Behaving in a manner cruel
      they call me insane
    a poet they will like to burn
      they not like a phoenix
    I will again and again return
They take me down
    downer and down
    their faces frown—I run to different grounds
    Where they chase me
me a lamb, chase these hounds

Sumirasko
153 Dt. 02.09.1993, 9.50 P.M.

Love's Dream

I have given the name of love
      love to this chaos 'My dove'
my heart is a moth's harte
        knows the burning art
     in your artistic loves' flame
it burns feels the pain insane
I feel the flower in every word
      feel the chirping of heavenly bird
feel the infinite innocent stream
        feel what you say not you mean
     and all in my poor love's dream
Which I see each moment each day
       or when in night's lap I lay
the cool breeze of love
      forever makes me drowsy
And I want to wake not
      What if the dream breaks
no promises, no oaths binds you 'my love'
      if you behave too serene
    on whose shoulders I will lean
      Let me sleep till death
   till death I will dream
       this love's dream

Sumirasko
154 Dt. 03.09.1993, 9.08 A.M.

The Silence

We speak, we try to deceive
        for a thousand hours stagnant
Our words at last want to creep
        And no one dares
Yet painful is this faithful silence
        there is a sublime voilence
you want to knew, the name of moon
        Know the Goddess of love
on painful grounds you stand
        crushed between belief and disbelief
Cannot bear this pain of yours
        you are like a simple child
Will make it today disappear
        not even leave it in a condition mild
After wards you can pretend
        you never were in pain
but your eyes today potray
        the vicious cain
my condition own is shaky
        find myself on lonely lane
this silence murders our soul
        will tell you who she is?
you can't take this more
        is boiling my harte's core

Sumirasko
158 Dt. 04.09.1993, 7.05 A.M.

Destiny

Weathered leaf flying in black wind
        falls one day
            in incertitude's final grave
    the grave nourishes a seed
        destiny answers the incarnation
      the seed grows to a tree or weed
Destiny that seed of life
       that shapes the future
     is helpless, the present flowing breeze
          Sweet breeze, if it confronts a gale
          if it turns a gale
      you can only weep and wail
Destiny she rules the world
      you never hear how she cries?
    a just ruler she is
      distribute unequally sorrows and joys
    for she is not blind
      creative souls she can find
   heap upon them mountain of sorrows
     break them completely
   break their faith in the morrow
Destined to feel great
they succumb easily to fate
their weathered faith like a leaf
    black nourishes the soul seed
sprouts to something
    a tree ultruistic or bitter wind
It's destiny not luck
     experiences of all fast life
helping in this present strife
    the vessel that floats on life's stream

She overturns
 soon is to drawn one, yet he feels water
  feels life
Destiny she first takes you down
  then takes high
Every good thing begins, creation of dawn begins
  in the darkness of night
 from chaos springs a star
   dancing bright

Sumirasko
155 Dt. 03.09.1993, 12.57 P.M.

No Panacea (Godesia)

Wherever I go, poverty I see
          Suffocation rants the air
misery is their life, carefree
          consciousness is lost
They are thirsty, feel not the thirst
          Their condition is abhominial
          They not (on) the higher planes
          and yet call themselves sanes
               A dumb is thirsty for making a Vibration
               A deaf for hearing a word
               A blind for seeing a ray
               handicapped for making a move
     Emotions deep, desire sleep
               makes them weep
helpless they know, something they miss
but these men who have all
          know not the supreme bliss
     for they have seen not a glimpse
               they have felt not the wind
          in deep coma, that is life's doom
               a carefree existence they seek
     bribing the priests, bribing their faith
               for a heavenly life after death
The germs of disease lies in God
          Godesia contagions kill the world
     Everywhere in the name of peace
               truth is scarified
                    by practical Godesia
     And yet, helpless I am
          oh! how desperate I feel
for the masses there is no pancea

Sumirasko
156 Dt. 03.09.1993, 3.23 P.M.

'Lean on me'

Burdenfull night hangs on your fate
      restless you feel each night late
you need a shoulder to lean on
      mine are not weak
you can lean—lean till dawn
Tormenting equivocations, burn your soul
      I will not warm my hands from a distance
    Crucifying emotions if you feel
          if you feel I lie
      unconditional love I can try
for trials succeed
      promises break
Lean on me you are a wreck
Prejudices if your mind breeds
      you will touch not a poor being
feel your harte, let it sing
      Lean on me roses I can bring
If you wait for a confession
      if you desire to have last say
reserve acceptance or rejection
      I give you this powerful right
      'Lean on me' without fright
'Lean on me' I am not stone
      I can feel your silence mean
for far too long, you have lived alone
      you have learn enough the harder way
      And, now I dare say
    'Lean on me'
      make my life worthy 'o fay'

Sumirasko
159 Dt. 04.09.1993, 7.55 P.M.

Diseased thoughts

Between belief and disbelief
        is crushed my harte
the devil torment this magical bard
       who needs love, fears rejection
today or tomorrow
       the Agony, the sorrow
In water confusion
     the flowers seem weathered
the rain that falls
     makes me shiver
So liquid I am
      can take no more liquidity
Whole night, I have longed for something
      is love my friend or something more
the lightening that strikes
      answers not my querry
I fear of losing you before I have you
     illogical conclusions I infer
     infer from enough premises
this grinding pain
     sees not virtues, cares only for vices
To you I call this nauseating dawn
     Save me, these deadly viruses
    to deadly thoughts I am too prone

Sumirasko
160 Dt. 04.09.1993, 8.45 A.M.

Express

When emotion is deep, express my love
   in heart core it they remain
      only a glimpse is seen above
    forces then sorrow, forces pain

II

The Nightingale feeds on glow-worms at night
   her voice so sonorous is inspired
         is inspired by my love's light
   If she gets none, if she is hungry
      She will turn pale
   even you will ail
     So express yourself my love
    express—she deserves
      express before all becomes
      still and stale
   you fail her, life me fails
      express before the breeze
the wind is taken out, out of love's sails

Sumirasko
161 Dt. 04.09.1993, 8.55 A.M.

The Snare

I can see you not in distress
the falling dew makes my life a mess
Want to show a genuine care
find that I myself in a snare
I wait upon speculations
      see not the path of love's stream
   in this ambiguous night
      helpless in heli stations
As impressions fall upon me
      the man in me is no where seen
   an innocent child crawls
      cries—know not reason
Instinctoid feelings grip me
     your gaze takes me down
   too bored you are
     bored with this child like clout
Boredom is pain, in your eyes I see
     locked is love, lost are keys
   too simple a duplicate I have
     but know not the use
       intelligent are the bees
who know a blooming flowers worth
     I hunt for paper flower on Earth
   this boredom kills your spirit
     woven is this snare, is well knit

Sumirasko
Dt. 04.09.1993, 9.10 P.M.

In the arms of emotion

Strange emotions, fearless devotion
    like slanting rain, eye's motion
  seizes me this sun's warmth
    that shines no where else
      only inside heart

The world is unaware
    nature shares this secret
the rain that falls today
    the occasional ray
  potrays the vision
    the vision of my lovely, lovely fay
Everything looks strange
    nature seems too deep
  my love has taken a sudden
      sudden new big leap
    the leaves of rose, the thorn that pricks
    the flower ah! beautiful
gives my soul, brimming with love
    a feeling joyful
  In the arms of emotion I awake
      oh! I love her for loving's sake

Sumirasko
164 Dt. 05.09.1993, 12.55 P.M.

When the bus ran away

(1983-86)

Those were days
      when flowers smelled strange
     leaves looked more green
when on trees a boy used to hang
     oh! those childhood swings
When the world was narrow
      narrow but too deep
Freedom I tasted
    when in my hands small
     a little power was vested
But one day, they took me to prison
     from forests I came to a small town
from birds and fouls nest
     to the cage of civilized hands
In an English school
    when they treated me like mule
    Teachers and classmates
      calling me rustic
       they made me always
        stand on a stool
they slapped, they carried like a savage
    For I never know their language
      they said 'you are a cabbage'
year after year they behaved tyrannically
    I cried, cried in pain
      no one came
a small boy crying alone
    for A, B, C, he had never known
never wanted to known
    just for a pretious show
   one day the harte, felt the tide
     the pain was disastrous
completely alone, the wanted to be hidden
     escapes revolt, no longer abide
the tread became slow

the love became long
resolution became, became too strange
when he reached the bus point
he saw the bus going, . . . going by
treaded back under a free sky
happy inside he went home
looking sad said to his mom
"It is a very inauspicious day
Mom the bus ran away

Sumirasko
Dt. 05.09.1993, 12.00 P.M.

Distant horizens come nigh

When distant horizons come nigh
    Love defines life origin
  we weep first—for the time first
    tears of real joy
  when sublime Earth is kissed
     kissed by the tender sky
  our love is as broad 'my girl'
    stars shine like pearl
  and though I wear no crown
   I feel like a king at least on Earth
you have got wings, I see you flying
   hear your fluttering voice
  is so intoxicating your spirit
   all life long for you I can compose lyric
My pen wants to see you not
   not again in pain
  too many agonies we both had
   now we must be pleasure clad
What I never dreamed 'my loved'
   that dream came true
  distant horizons have come nigh
   Love we have got in lien

Sumirasko
166 Dt. 05.09.1993, 02.56 P.M.

The Square

All along my tread was alone
no voice ever called
all along—all day long
I have longed for someone
on square I waited
in painest indecision
people came and passed
none saved me from the prison
I knew I had something more
cannot mould myself in their mould
I rebelled—they laughed scornfully
my courage never left made me bold
Until you came from direction east
so blind I was to ray
at first I shivered 'o fay'
yet a hope deep inside lay
Weary I was forever, weary you no more
by destined chance we have met on the square
now we move ahead on one path
for we share the same feeling
from this square our life begins

Sumirasko
167 Dt. 05.09.1993, 06.00 P.M.

The anabolic ambit

by Alexander Raskolinikov

Momentry flashes of deep insight
illuminates the horizons of mist sky
　　　　But it Evaporates—so calmly, so quickly
　　　　it is difficult to grasp the reality
　　　　The furious sun checks its weak light
　　　　While the selenian sinwt dominates
　　　　　　　　　—the rest of the night
No matter how fast the gale ransacked
his castle remained safe and unmatched
But he knew it himself what a strange surprise?
On top floor he slept, while the bottom remained forbidden
forgotten and fortified
years passed and yet nothing changed
But a night in July and the chapter one took over
from the formidable gale
Such an impact it had that the foundation
creaked, swerved and was about to fail
Fortuitously he awoke and fought with fortitude
against the storm in veil
　　　　The dawn came—he was wide awake
　　　　he glanced at the castle with awe struck gaze
　　　　Where he lived—for how many year's he could not tell
　　　　The painting's on the wall—so near and yet so pale
　　　　Perhaps he needed time to adjust to the new laws
　　　　that nature had revealed with such flair
A sudden urge of re-discovery took him to the bottom
Where half-becked brickes, medieval furnishing and some
Magic potion—lied behind a bolted door
with a few holes
The adrenalin pumped up—the door went down
he found a staircase waiting perhaps for a crown

The beautiful vaulted room looked for
more enchanting the truth
the walls well decorated but alas! for the ancient Indians
the floor was made of stones unsuitable
for a Prometheus
He paced up and down for the sake of the crown
                    new found noun
    and a stone helped him in getting down

Sumirasko
3/year 1991

Insecurity

I

I am a poet of minute or two
        peradventure in a pensive mood
you will forget in a day
        like you all forget the morning dew
My name will not cloud the sky
        emotions will die insane
    for this is a real world
            you want a real rain
And someday the wind of affection will cease
            the weather will change morrow
    my voice will seem cursed
            fake my dreamy sorrow
This is a real world
        to me it seems quite ill
    you all will blind me if I keep my view
        blind for a real life thrill
I will live like a vegetable green
        from every eye unseen
    until dumped in a waste box
        in a minute or two as my genius last
For this is a momentary world
        in a moment you can forget
    now you adore, admire
        in the moment next devilishly hate

II

My own words eat me savagely
        too gruesome is this insecurity
    there is no spirit on which I can lean
        my blood gets thinner and thin
    Wherever I see I just don't fit
            in any mould of whatever shape
        for I just can't, I just can't
            imitate like an ape
    Too bloody is the philosopher in me

Spills my blood, my clothes drip
Shivers each strand, each hair in misery
And you close your eyes, overlook don't see
The fault is not yours if I swoon
if mine is the unseen ugly moon
It's bloody insecurity, chopping me into pieces
Showering bitter kisses, myriad verses
Verses that give you a heavenly delight
make my yoke double not light
yet if I ever find a grave, I pray this
the world forgets my name—my verse don't miss
For, they are real lightening that emanate
fall upon you or light your path
I am just a suffering black virtual cloud
thundering in your ears loud
My cry is impalpable, so you don't hear
but recorded present please don't tear
Without my name they will not hurt you
yet they will have this blood like hue

Sumirasko
122 Dt. 29.08.1993, 5.20 P.M.

The Feminine Principle

Feminine principle have you ever heard about
  am a strong man I have some clout
  All world bows in front of them
    Yet I am pretty numb for them
   So I knew a little secret
     which is rather sacred
   When you want to get in
      touch with unreality
    go to a woman
when you hunt for some want on sensuality
  pay a visit
    it will be a treat
  of you are rather maternal
     rest under her bower
  the securest place
    it's an inferior, its complex
For all woman do, is to divert and entertain
  one thousand thirty million miles
     away from reality
   you fly with them
      when the spell is over
  the time period is hundred and eight years
the principle you know minutely
   women are all peers
  on her finger spins the world
  instruments of the herd to wield itself
  proving healing balm to violent selves
    until their violence ebbs

Sumirasko
283 Dt. 20.09.1993, 5.50 P.M.

Perfect Indecision

Harte? this panting Harte
                that breathes your fragrance
            and eyes that see you stare
        want to see everywhere only your face
        Mine eyes! they potray what desperation
Tears oh! these wild tears
                of pain or of pleasure
    or, at once of both
            tears that flow
                flow like a sweet stream
    fall like rain
                what deadly equivocations
        Tread OH? quick tread
            Covering love's distance
        fumbling, falling, standing
            faults mending
        in glow worm's light seeing
            what's their destination?
Soul OH! poor soul
Courageless, helpless, guileless
            just charmed, just alarmed
        at every trifle danger
                yet full of love
                    what devotion
I the owner of all these
                know that I just love
        Know I wait for your word
                or wait for a word from within
            within myself I mean
                what indecision!

Sumirasko
255 Dt. 17.09.1993, 2.30 P.M.

My Monalisa

My Maiden is a living Monalisa
    not a stone sculpture but a breathing beauty
    excelling all that is past
            prevailing o'er future
in innocence, in devotion, in faith, in love
      in all, is her harte above
    And OH! that sweet voice
       what sugar cubes! what divine joy
Just see her rare form and strange hues
          what chisel can stone can bestow
her hue that beats the moon lit snow
none can surpass in front of her that I know
      Time again will not claps its hand
moon and snow will never again feel pride
      of being compared with my mistress light
    her strange hue
       is a rare delight
     all things rare are eternized
       My Monalisa too is immortalized

Sumirasko
253 Dt. 17.08.1993, 12.00 A.M.

31

City to Village and Sacrilege

Yea! I have made this, is a Sacrilege
     for you aren't with me my love
        only next to hell is this village
Though the air clean, my breath is heavy
     though here peace reigns, my harte is noisy
        beats so loud, so loud it cries
        is hungry for your sweet voice
OH! trapped I am, alone here
     amidst nature mirthful
     the shining moon looks dull
     waking stars asleep
I want to but could not weep
     The moth dies too here
as in the city O 'Dear'
     the same flame burns everywhere
        the same face—no other is for me
        I see not the village fairy
Village is better then city I agree
but my senses are with you my love
I am 'deaf' 'blind' 'dumb' disabled here
     how can I enjoy nature carefree?
Form city to village is a way long
each day for you I long
     for to you I be long
not to any village, not to any city
     I wait but how long?
Destiny upon me, have some pity
even an hour is a wait too long
     I care not for the village deity
     I wish to see, I wish to pray to
        my breathing beauty

Sumirasko
227 Dt. 13.09.1993, 11.00 A.M.

Vision

Blurred faces in smoky day
      burning eyes perceive
not that blue cool light
      that shines the sky
or that serene grace
      that shines in her face
Do blind me, I will see this no more
     I close my eyes day run wildly
run bring the unblemished night
     neither moon nor stars or clouds bright
Without her . . . at a distance
        need not any sight
           any vision
any waking dream, come not nigh
      come I scream
until I am with her
      until I see her
Kind she is, without any pray
        She will lend me a ray
      for she is 'my fay'
only thou will I see again
        the poetry in nature
     the poetess with her living pen
      the faces and their expression
till thou lost is my acumen
       my vision

Sumirasko
228 Dt. 13.09.1993, 12.30 A.M.

On Peace

Peace a cursed word
    in the common dictionary of the herd
who know only grave yard stillness
    grave yard peace
      have never felt the living tranquility
    that seeps drop by drop
      from within
    in a mind tranquil
  Where will thou search for peace
      in richness
Nay the rich men suffer more
      for reaped prematurely, is teared
        one belief 'I will be happy if I am rich'
    yet you must find it there
      there is no escape
    the immaterial lotus of peace living
      proliferates in the dirty material lake
  The poor can never understand
      Why the rich suffer
But I know "on a mental plane
      empty is their coffer"
from that turmoil alone springs neo tranquility
    Poor's peace is but grave yard ambiguity
Peace is not the absence of war
Peace is not the absence of pain
is inner tranquility, ecstasy blissful rain

Sumirasko
229 Dt. 13.09.1993, 2.20 P.M.

The Diary

Is haunting me an unseen diary
someone is its owner and the owner is killed
while I am entirely revealed
           She is entirely concealed
      And while she knows each
           fragment of my personality
      Knows fully my integrity
           I know nothing, entirely in dark
      And this isn't justice
Awkward I feel OH! How will I deal
         the passion that I too know her
         as she knows me
           me it will kill
There are only dark clouds here
         the sky is concealed
there are only dark clouds here
         the sky is concealed
      there are no answers
           only endless querries
And all for that diary
Suffocations I feel in this smother
        I stand so close and know
           not the other
A thing concealed imparts pain
        but a self concealed is life's bane
when you yourself stand bore
        see nothing but only empty stare
The pages of her life If I can read
if I share her pain if I know her seed
      if only if I am so fortunate
         fortunate to understand her nature
   will thank her

Her diary for me is a priceless jewel
her denial is a death nail
Words written—a true vision, her vision
I will decipher more dexterously
then I ever deciphered any constitution
But today my verses are revealed
her words conceal
And I, I request 'o owner don't
be so skilled'

Sumirasko
252 Dt. 17.09.1993, 11.30 P.M.

Recollected Ecstasy

Unequal is my breath, mind is empty
thoughts today elude
      Sweat cools the forehead
birds voice enters straight
    into the living fire
that burns inside
    My eyes closed today see light
feel the stillness that resides
      in each body pore
    burning in cool blue light
      that surrounds
Now I hear nothing
    now I feel nothing but delight
And delight is not unusual
    is too simple humane and simple
yet I call it ecstasy
    the feeling is of being light
Now I feel nothing
    it's the supreme height

II

I find no images
    yet I will describe
from within a power filled
    filled my empty mind
    the world seemed joyful, blissful, warm and kind
    then dissolved to blankness
      pure serenes

Sumirasko
230 Dt. 13.09.1993, 3.15 P.M.

Love is Salvation

OH! I am here at last
    in this lighted room
the fan that revolves overhead
    the air that sweeps my bare feat
the pen that is in my hand
    And oh! the music so sweet
    back to home
      has returned this spirit
For two long days it roamed in wilderness
    amid it nature plenty
    yet longed, for what it had left
      longed for that sweet voice
    Longed for some face angelic
      in which bloom roses and lilac
    At best back, it rises in love
    rises above
    what more nature can bestow
And what more beatific vision it has to show
    All is pale in front of her
the spirit has returned home
    to living nature that shins in her
    No where else is its destination
    only near to love—for love is salvation

Sumirasko
231 Dt. 14.09.1993, 01.00 P.M.

January

She wears that smile
    my spirit in a bodily form
Wears that face
    this life's incarnation
    Paragon of beauty
    is my January
Thought the name is Psudo
    here upon the green meadow
    When the first ray falls
    my harte strolls
    a voice from within
    whispers softly
    Whisper's January
in the voice I hear her echo
    so I call her so
She by heavens grace
    is always first
    a soul perpetual, always new
    needs not the fabulous mayden'
or the human jewellery
    for herself is a priceless jewel
    My January
with a grace like dawn
    unlike it perpetual happiness
of the first month, first morn

Sumirasko
230 Dt. 14.09.1993, 2.06 P.M.

Conquest

In a great world
     a trifle word
yet one I appreciate
    out of jealousy, out of envy
tomorrow I can hate
    for today I can conquer
rule over entire nature
    from a yellow leaf to forests green
    from dark dusk to golden morn
today I sit on the throne
    wear a crown sovereign
with a pen in my hand, a blank paper
    'I paint man's nature'
a full moon, not only the lighted half
    I paint too the other dark
Here I see I am ahead
     only one in the race
in the entire human race
    who appreciates baseness

Sumirasko
234 Dt. 14.09.1993, 4.15 P.M.

Interrogated

It was a cool waiting night
    wait that stops or kills the watch
  a man smoking stood near a rich gate
    alone early night both spread her quiteness
Poorly dressed yet not so poor
    within waited a harte heavy
  outside a rich gate, weaving a verse
    waited for some one
      some square mate
The stars were all on strike
    the moon behind the veil
  impatient walked to and fro
    the man awaiting male
Apparations sneaked in from around the corner
    I saw him—he was like a mourner
  his intuition flied in black sky
    said within if I be interrogated I die
Too short his length, dwarf his height
    seized him unusual fright
  with every tread that came close
    Poetry turned prose
Music turned in a wild uproar
    as they passed on—he got some relief
  as they turned fired a salvo
    what is your identity
      shaken was his belief
'O Man' 'o man' who once dissented
    from lining up in a queue
  now interrogated—I saw condition
    OH! How people chew
As he thought, read their thoughts
    felt their consciousness
  infernal ideas stuffed their mind
for he stood outside a rich gate
    only his poor clothes they could find

And what his colour, what his emotion
　　　like a stick wavering, a cheap stick
for a moment he felt his abyss
　　　felt his identity falling in

Interrogation the question of identity
　　　'Eternal no' he saw for a brevity
a star single fell from sky broke the strive
　　　his throats uttered a helpless cry
he felt his greatness—was a lie
A big Zero outside a rich gate
　　　meaningless existence
　　　　　　closed fate

Sumirasko
233 Dt. 14.09.1993, 3.21 P.M.

The Man

On muddy village road
 a man strolls
his name unknown, his face known
 strange eyes, keen treating sight
 ears too keen and lips amazing
 with those very lips
 with village dogs he talks
alleges he solves their problem
 knows each by name
And when a bird cries on the bough
 or a fowl sings
 he talks and sings—a strange being
 He is a man who knows the extremes
 in rage he stones the village chief
 his blood then flows in muddy lanes
 Will you call him sane?
 though his is the label of being insane?
Whatever the village men say
 Whatever is your verdict
 I hear the village wind
 I hear the axe like lightening
 and all nature that hails pure will natural
 he is a man living
 amidst men dead virtual
 I the sole keeper of truth can
 label him not
 yea! you call him insane
 Just because he is not of your veins
Meek, dwarf, civilized, secured sane
 he is the real man, if he be Insane
 in reaction as a judge
My verdict is "All real men are insane"
 sane but shadows of their selves
 Shadows, empty, insane

Sumirasko
235 Dt. 14.09.1993, 5.36 P.M.

Borrowed thoughts

I am a college youth
       I tell thee, I am blind
and dumb, deaf and disabled
       My world is some one else's world
My words all borrowed
I see only other's vision
I hear only what men speak
         in their high class diction
       I take more interest in their fiction
My father commanded once
         'there is God'
       I accepted simply, gave no second thought
       And some one said 'the Earth is round'
       to his words instantly I was bound
'This is wrong, that is right'
       all I devoured, all lessons light
And when now my lips utter
       they imitate those very lessons
When I see 'I perceive those very visions'
       when I hear 'I hear only those passages'
         Words of sages
When I walk 'I tread on those very known lanes'
       Life is so easy, perfect security
         OH! Thinking is a bore
see I hold the crutch of borrowed thoughts
like a parasite I feed on them
       they end not—eternal food
       none can say I am hungry
       I am a topper of my university
Borrowed thoughts
       Why 'O' Poet your are angry

Borrow from me some
    Borrow my world
Borrow, speak what they teach
    that have come down to me
'strength is unity' 'unity is in the herd'

Sumirasko
248 Dt. 16.09.1993, 2.20 P.M.

Unnatural Love

O graceful beauty
        moon shining in my harte's sky
a cloud single eclipses you
        when will it drift
    this veil will lift
        And I will see thou—a living
And share with thou that high romance
        When will change this peculiar stance
An unusual feature
            never read such escapades
        never in worlds literature
have seen not such seems in nature
        a single cloud eclipsing man
    But in betwixt us, its a practical reality
Tell me when this unnatural love 'O Kind'
        will reveal itself, will change the scene
    too desperate I am
        Answer me 'when this eclipse will end

Sumirasko
247 Dt. 16.09.1993, 1.50 P.M.

Unmarked Harte

'O Prithee'
My harte is an empty ocean
    with love come, fall like first rain
With lightening like love
    fill it with fiery devotion
'O Dame'
My mind recoils in equivocations
    come with a message clear
clean up the woods 'o dear'
    make my fear a strength
        sow a grain of faith
    impart it a tranquil state
'O heavenly light'
    Bestow upon me a single ray
        from heavens come down 'o fay'
    Make my days, a heavenly feast
        at night hold me tight
    give me light, I could see my shadow
        the darkest facets, the primal ego
'O friend'
    If you find me unworthy
make my pain, your pleasure instead
And here I will lie with an empty ocean
with tormenting equivocations in dark
feel each moment, painful death stark
    if you believe not my verses
        there is no other way
    I am not a labelled lover
        on my harte there is no mark

Sumirasko
243 Dt. 15.09.1993, 4.32 P.M.

On Morality and Mortality

Huge walls of stone erected
        between persons
     convicted—to a stone like life
  In front of God's palace
     stad these beggars
Wearing a shining gold guise
     deep down cheap stone lies
God's word—the full stop
     faith—a dangerous word
morality—instrument to weild the herd
     and ah! the wonder man, the miracle man
Chirst says so
       hear my voice and I will give the food
       Salvation—on this word they stand
Chirst is a tiger, meek are the lamb
      jungle rules here apply
  on this planet, each generation
        Each herd dies
    devoured by the son of God
       that moral man
       that miracle man
  or by men like him of other faith
     ruling their princly forest states
Moral tigers freely roam
     certified morality, a moral code
not challenged by fearful masses
     is their throne
They have grabbed power
     other men rule, in their name
each priest, each father, each mother
     living in moral temples or treading on moral lanes
Beasts are here amidst us
     moral beasts, morality is their weapon
     to subdue and we assist
     they kill us before death
yet happily we present garlands or wreath

And morality we preserve, mortality we get
    Ah! for they are our elders
        chained are our thoughts
Which little by little tiger feed
        and what is left
    is thrown to the vultures
        Death—eats the rotten meat
And that surely is salvation
first to Tiger, than to vulture
        we promise moral devotion
we break no oath, break, no duty
gloriously we serve morality
        And that is all—No more is time
    for we are lost in mortality
        hear the death call, here the chime

Sumirasko
242 Dt. 15.09.1993, 3.15 P.M.

Perfume

Scared eyes behold everywhere
        a snare
      see the past—a burning flare
            the future seems a blanket dark
        only a blind stare
And now my harte is so full of love
        yet is so full of filthy unreason
Can make no promises
          can take not a decision
Till the crack of dawn
              it weaves your fancy
        like leaves, drops of dens
            that scatter in the breeze
      fear breaks every fancy
              yet I can live not in reality
Will you help me love
        will you fragrance, my soul
a soul that is full of gloom
        Each day fears doom
    Will you shine on it like moon
          the filthy harte, a withered harte
              will you perfume?
        soon my love . . . . soon

Sumirasko
241 Dt. 15.09.1993, 1.40 P.M.

Complete Dependence

Ensconced in pain, esteemed in snore
I search for love, flinging my harte
     in you I search 'O fair'
  I flagellate myself not
     this inflection both spread
  which doubts the reality
     rejection I dread
  when I show my desperate harte
      I fear this to be lure a bait
    I fear the change of trapping will
       fall upon one
  Yet, I am myself trapped
My harte now is an your very hands
    crush it under your feet
      or break it in you palms
  or perfect it, apply healing balms
     it's for you to take a decision
       leave me or take me out
         out of this prision
I lean upon your tender shoulders
    shrug me off or let me sleep
      under shadows of silky tress
  a weary bed-ridden patient
        in distress
    leaves all upon you
      'O mistress'

Sumirasko
239 Dt. 16.09.1993, 3.00 P.M.

Living Lucy

I have given you thousands of name
    baptized 'your spirit' many times
    'rose' 'fay' cindrella, January
    And my harte full of mirth
              today makes merry
    For at last I have immortalized you
        given you your true nature
            'O immortal spirit'
    Thou were never constructed
        never by that cheap 'God'
        So, many forms only I gave you
        'without any informal talk
        In the present you belong to me
           in future you will reign supreme
        o'ver these hartes that cherish poetry
            those priceless, ageless harte
        o'ver many a centuries
Thou will be a brimming river
        Lucy was only a tributary
    for no one loved anyone so much
        in love no one composed so many verses
Without revealing, Thou have achieved this feat
        'O' immortal spirit, Hail to thee
    Today I call you my love
        baptize you, give a name new
            you aren't emphatically a fancy
        you are a 'living Lucy'

Sumirasko
251 Dt. 16.09.1993, 5.30 P.M.

The Feminine Principle

Feminine principle have you ever
         heard about
    'am a strong man I have
                  some clout
'All world bows in front of them'
            yet I am pretty numb for them
         so I know a little secret
which is rather sacred
         When you want to get in
                  touch with unreality
            go to woman
         when you hunt for some wait
                        on sensuality
         pay a visit
         it will be a treat
         if you are rather maternal
                  rest under her bower
         the securest place
            it's an inferior, it's complex
For all women do is to divert and entertain
            one thousand thirty million miles away from reality
            you fly with them
               when the spell is over
            the time period is hundred and eight years
         the principle you know minutely
                  women are all peers
         on her finger spins the world
         Instruments of the herd to weild itself
      proving healing balm to
                     violent selves
            until their violence ebbs

Sumirasko
283 Dt. 20.09.1993, 5.50 P.M.

Awake

Awake, now awake
>> once more I bang your ear drums
> be no more deaf
See, the golden morn shining
> see the volcanoes errupting
OH! actors sleeping
>> When will the drama begin?
>> Sleep no more fulfill the stage
What dream castles you build
>> eternal dream, sweet dream
> dream OH! dream at least once
> originally think
> escape not, life isn't a burden
Alas! no more material dreams
> know yourself, first find self
> then if need be
>> burst for power and pay
Mutilate your bodies
> mutilate your mind
for breaking sleep
> use instruments of any kind
And here I call at the top of my voice
> awake or you be wreck
>> a grave yard's corpse
> a grave yard stone
awake! the old life is spent, a new life begins
>> a gloomy era is over, a trumphant
> verily not even I can teach
>> only your spirit
>>> that will arise from within

No teacher, no prophet is more faithful
    than an awakened voice
        and voices are two
    awake, take delight in their duel
        leave everything upon the voices
        don't discriminate between virtues and vices
        in short—make no choices
    until the choice arises from within
        you understand not, scratch not your head
        first awake and you will know what
                I mean.

Sumirasko
256 Dt. 17.09.1993, 3.10 P.M.

On Personal Liberty

Be so literal as to discuss it
       its a seed that must be sown
    What if society is to moon
Personal liberty must not be imported
         but snatched by men undaunted
     It's the most potent power of destruction
           most potent too for creation
        Society must not groom any plant
          to its likes
     but let it groom naturally even if
            it is cactus with thorny spikes
      it must believe in diversity not unity
         bear eccentricity
    Such personal liberty is like natural moon
       the sun, the genius is born
      men are unequal, equality is false
      personal liberty is a fruit
         not all can enjoy
       only at this moment in history
         rebellious men not coy
And when we say we are free, we err
    for our choices are customary
we always sccumb, we mostly confirm
     use not our intellect
take prime decisions under pressure
      So, is reduced our strature
We lead life as other's wish
       in our way, life we never kiss
in short we lead not our kind of life
but some one elses
    a number of elses
We have lost our, but wear
        too many faces

And that is not personal liberty
        Just ambiguity and conformity
The way to real liberty is thorny
           Sarcasms, curses, stares too many
     but once you get
          even if they fume and fret
   liberty's esteem will save your spirit
you will know a base truth
       leading such a life is a true merit

Sumirasko
258 Dt. 17.09.1993, 6.00 P.M.

Life and Death

Someone calls me
        I hear clearly
    but I see not the face
        never heard any skylark singing
    never heard its mirthful strain
the call seems from within
        it's faithful death calling
           Death is within
    Each cell treasures it
        Each drop of blood nourishes
the call is now louder and louder
        faithless life shivers
    I' who is above life and death
      above garlands and wreath
    have seen life, heard death
      a desire is to see it
      to see is to die
investigate fully
      Does death too lie?
        like life has
for none of my fault
      She has betrayed twice
first made me see a mirage
        give an empty hope
then left in darkness alone
      alone to grope
She deceived me twice
        is Death comfortably nice

And is it really soothing
    can its rough hand soothe me
Can it bear sweet fruits
    Can its loud call awake me
Life has made me drowsy
it's call I hear—It's call is so dear
    still there is some fear
in my eyes there is a drop of tear
    a tear shed in life's love
    a drop shed in death's welcome

I
Life has betrayed, death comes
it calls me, I have no energy
    static I am, can not chose one

Sumirasko
268 Dt. 18.09.1993, 4.15 P.M.

The Drunkard

OH! this love's deep drink
        I have swallowed many virtual beings
And today I feel
        for real love still I beg
No money I have to buy love
        Yea! it can be bought
My soul an addict
        is a burning coal hot
No power I have to command anyone
        why anyone will succumb?
Why you will succumb
        hear my cries, be numb
Each drop of blood clamours
        for that elixir
if not pure, will settle for that
        crude mixture
But money I have not
        for buying even crude love
and money is a primary condition
        for even you for every one
So, a drunk and faces damnation
And when I die, if you dig my grave
        write an epitaph
bear the little cost or collect some aid
        whatever men may think
Write only 'Here a thirsty drunkard is laid'
        And thou can celebrate my ill-reputation
and thou can buy love's ocean
        satiate your thirst life long
A drunkard's grave will only potray
        Life long dark days—not a ray
With thirst too deep I will die
        for love I could not buy

And you will give it not face of cost
      your love is a pearl, it has to be bought
   A thirsty man is a mocking sight
     So until I die—take in me delight
       for I am condemned to be forever thirsty
      Satiations is only your birth right

Sumirasko
262 Dt. 18.09.1993, 1.20 P.M.

Destiny

Yea! I myself command my destiny
    and I am above
  with such skill, my path I chose
    from 'chaos' a dancing star rose
The world sees not, it shows their cowardice
    fear a star too joyously bright
      will blind
  yea! they analyse with a closed mind
  I made myself fall, from great heights
    ah! what healthy diets
    an inner strength, too week is steel
      for it can't know itself, can't feel
Now, no more I need to jump down
    in this black hungry town
    forever on top, the test of will is over
    a new man has taken over
For the last climb was a classical affair
    the last fall lead to quagmaire
Out of this ditch, no one can take me down
    hollow men in stuffed towns
  let them frown, I have found destination
    carved myself, my destiny
      found salvation

Sumirasko
282, Dt. 20.09.1993, 4.36 P.M.

Cold Fusion

Inside me the impossible has happened
    shock therapy has deepened
now every cell thinks, feels
    from such heights I fell
that fear itself is killed
    is no more
eloquence in words
    of this happiness is above
No more I analyse, accept the whole
    the whole self from head to toe
    shivering in joy
And I know for sure, others I don't need
    not even birds and bee
    for all are . . . . all are in me
the veil is torned, now I can see
I can see nothing, just feel
    the consciousness merging becoming one
Mystical cold fusion, no more friction
    no more momentary
no mere a recollection
    but eternal salvation
    joyous joy, joyous joy
    an eversible phenomena
    who can destroy?

Sumirasko
281, Dt. 20.09.1993, 4.10 P.M.

Rupturns Mirth

From a burning hearth
        has sprung this rapturous mirth
My body frail is too strong
        my spirit laughs loudly
People all around today stare
            my lighted face looks fair
    my laughter echoes inside
        who today me can divide
    Who is so foolish as to despise
            who can despise
        who cares abouts virtues and vice
            it's so nice, so very nice
    Heaven and Earth dance with joy
            have been foiled a those secret plays
        just by this inner tranquility
            is no more alive any ambiguity
    That load of disease has decomposed
            my face is verily composed
        rupturous mirth has intensity such
            it needs not any crutch
My eyes that gleam, perceive no gloom
        everywhere flowers bloom
    living flowers, living fragrances
        all a living boon

Sumirasko
280 Dt. 20.09.1993, 3.55 P.M.

Spiritual Leisure

Happiness without measure
     just feasting upon pleasure
so near to my God
     feelings they just trod
without any support to lean
     OH! my senses are so keen
in silence, in stillness there is a great depth
     I see life is unlike flowing lethe
It's a stream reflecting sun beam
     grace of eternal spirit
the stream ends, remains
     my eternal merit
Buds that never open
     and flowers that fail
Can make life misery
     can make spirit cloudy
But I see, through that cloud
     the spirit spinning as before
spiritual leisure all around
     to Ecstasy bound
Who now needs anyone
What recognition and what throne
When deepest pain hath given fruit
     to leisure in past unknown

Sumirasko
279 Dt. 20.09.1993, 8.40 P.M.

Joyful Hate

Joyous hate is now my mate
it's not ecstasy
        but a power giving state
I hate the wind, I hate the bind
all that I loved, now I hate
        it's their fate
What's this alchemey
        like a pharoh I feel
yet, I hate my mummy
     Ah! what play of words
        too bitter a curd
I feel superior
        everyone else inferior
            inferior of the herd
What gold can buy
      such universal enjoyment
what love can surpass
     this savage merriment
a sublime agreement
       with oneself
     joyous hate
       not a drop of remorse
each face looks filthy
       each man a racing horse
   I hate filthy looks, racing horses
ah! how joyous hate carrases
      Satiates love's thirst
   hate joyful is a step ahead of love
      Please no one disturb
     it's a great herb

Sumirasko
278 Dt. 20.09.1993, 2.40 P.M.

The Liar

Allegations he faces, pinching allegations
      some one labelled him 'a liar'
   scornful expression
     now eats his harte
Vehemence, spasms quivers each cell
    how the person dared
  a simple humble being
      OH! how salvos she fired
And what made her think so
OH! what confused brain
Tell her anyone, life isn't a game
OH! such shallow understanding
      I had overestimated her
Can never understand 'what liar means'
    on a plane superior
Hell beat on generalizing
    what essentially is particular
Hell bent on demoralizing
    when I know not any morals
yea! I feel pain and vehemence
Vehemence out classes pain
    OH! what mercy she hath bestowed
    OH! what name
a voice somewhere grows louder
     'Calling fairwell Dame'
Vehemence tears every veil
   it was all a
      fairy tale, fantasy
now in self–love I see it is all
   such mess I don't like messy
    My benovalence goes on strike

Sumirasko
277 Dt. 19.09.1993, 2.15 P.M.

SUMIRASKO

Sandwitched

Between him and her
Between two loaves of bread
        I reside I dread
                one loves, the other hates
                one inspires, the other prespires
                one takes high, the other low
                one says yes, the other 'No'
both so near, both so dear
        in my eyes, well tears
    too great a pressure
                breaks my spine
    too balanced am I, same am I
                but fed up with this
        balancing act of mine
Destiny why did you brought me into . . . . .
no more torment
        play some wild tricks
take me out
        for, too gruesome is this unseen bout
My heart is already weak, some how stiched
        Can no more afford
                afford to be sandwitched

Sumirasko
271 Dt. 19.09.1993, 11.00 A.M.

Round the clock

I

Day and night I just shiver to think
OH! if she ever cast me off her eyes
    the lamp of my life that slowly diminishing
    OH! if this sorrowful breeze finally extinguishes

II

Day and night I have just shrank thinking
half her eyes have cast me off
the lamp of my life nears extinction
this sorrowful blizzard is too fast for diction

Sumirasko
269 Dt. 18.09.1993, 8.00 P.M.

Just Vainful

Back to square one
I have won again
this prized pain
ah! this life's game
    Defeat is victory
    falling stars merge in Earth
        Earth she makes merry
        Bursts out in a rupturous mirth
    Edifices when fall
    ah! its great fun
    at a collosal universe
    you stare in return
Every breeze carries venom
        Every heavenly light darkness
    you question yourself? Shaken is your faith
      in a big universe completely alone
        you dance not on the stone sabbath
You know they love, they admire, they adore
    when you fall it seems
      they laugh, they hate, they scorn
You see not the morn
      completely forlorn
O innocent swallow caged in sorrowness
      Just know their trifleness
    their shallowness
      break free alone
        non will help
          on them not lean
they are dead
      stones already in grave laid

Can only break a living
    cannot make
there is nothing at stake
    there is no comparison
    all are just fake
Make no efforts to move again
tread not night long on any lane
it's just vain
no one will feel your pain

Sumirasko
272 Dt. 19.09.1993, 12.45 A.M.

The Man

The man a complex being
        a bundle of complex emotions
    somehow held
        to life nailed
The man oh! man
      like a star which can fall
any moment
      Man—full of love, full of gall
    rupturous mirth and violent hearth
        OH! how he treads on Earth
    or flies in open sky
        and OH! how he does lie
A miraculous species
        a puzzling engima
    some roses he treasures
        some throws on the grave
    save voices he likes
        some he merciful hates
      OH! what dreadful tastes
Misconceptions light his night
        illusions his day
    plays a trifle vicious game
      OH! the shame
    Man isn't human
        but a bundle of maneuvering acumens

A mixture of love and venom
a duel of mind and harte
somehow fastened together
when string breaks, awaits grave
the rose waits
rose that exemplifies present's beauty
exemplified him some day
is laid on his grave
all is forgotten, his love and rage
yea! Man is always an empty page

Sumirasko
270 Dt. 19.09.1993, 9.15 A.M.

OHIO

Which harte breaks, he cries ohio
    when love swells
in deep sorrow compounded
    having no morrow
When they ebb, sings a sad number
    in his rustic fashioned voice
      never is his the dice
And when he sings
    on broken roads or in a weathered meadow
Sings with a cut throat
    at the end he cries 'OHIO'
He knows not what he cries
    yet in that cry half his soul dies
    it seems to me a call in Desperado
    each day he cries 'OHIO'
Each moment in an eternal love's net
    'OHIO' is suffocating I bet
No one listens, even I speculate
      clearly don't know
    Why so mournfully he cries OHIO

Sumirasko
261 Dt. 18.09.1993, 12.20 P.M.

Goddess of Love

There is a grace in her steps
for me they pave new ways
Each tread makes me light
the stars above really shine bright
clothed in moon's milky ray
When she stands on the sand
a living goddess is she
in her devotion my breaths pray
I kneel before her in ecstasy
just looking at her
at her lips saying not a word, mute
while wind and waves play for her the flute
on such nights my goddess is alive
some say she is but trivial clay
but nature seems to know her spiritual halo
together to the Goddess of love we pray

Sumirasko
145 Dt. 01.09.1993, 8.20 P.M.

Effort

This a feverish fever
a deadly anger
against myself, against all
caught again in a snare
     I am really bare
Clouds come and rain today
rain until the Earth is swept away
Make the clime so dark
not a ray can escape
     I will cry not again
     'stop O Rain'
And wind sweep the entire globe
tides come and devour Earth
Demons today make mirth
     add me to your group
and let me clamour wildly
     add me to baseness
Let my pleasure be their restlessness
     And sun I command thee
     Yea! I command thee
     never come again
out . . . out of this hungry land
     And 'fay' thou are really made of clay
in anger I can break, run away

None come near me to whisper you are insane
Sour not my soul by request up Behave
like a man
its sourness is without limits
it has just viciousness, demerits
I will never again beg for love
never again request a dove
'o wind' 'o rain' 'o tide' 'o sun'
just seed out life and love
seed out Earth and heaven
all ashes in urn
and there will be no stone
I will hunt not for love and care
there will none of beauty's daughter
other then my own soul fair

Sumirasko
268 Dt. 18.09.1993, 2.20 P.M.

Too Deep

I have treaded in too deep
    too deep in her love's ocean
  a virtual ocean
    can come not back
    Cannot back track
only drown in my tears real
    OH! I was a thief par excellence
  but her harte I could not steal
Eternal failure too deep
  my genius weeps
there is none to measure it
  a shining gold—blind is my fay
Unlike Black I am not so fortunate
  no girl will ever hold me
if even she can't—none will ever love me
This is a different realm
  of poetry and true love
  Can feel not both 'My dove'
    has wings but cannot fly so high
under material gravity or in gold cage
  is content, too deep is this realm
  too deep isn't her bent
  And too deep is my lament
I want to take her to those planes
Where too deep is life
  And she is content, with hovering like butterfly
  on the surface
  then be a secured wife!

She will repent, a repentance too deep
    will seize when every thing is lost
      OH! will she, will sleep all life?
this pain is roasting me alive
And this I say to her, don't err
       too deep will be the wound
    burn your intuition, burn your emotion
      in love's deep fire
    before I meet my second death
before you weigh me, against riches
      or condition any I fulfill not
    And you will know you have riches
    but a soul which really loves
       you love not
Too deep is my fear of being despised
remember . . . . remember my advice
    I want a hand, casually you don't take
and if you want me, sacrifices you make
     or else sacrifice me
      for a secured life
too deep is my blood's hue
       kill from a distance
    your rich clothes it can stain
    a stain too deep
pain will devour—for you me slightly love
    there will be no o'er leap

Sumirasko
260 Dt. 18.09.1993, 11.15 P.M.

Intermission

OH! this love
    like a thorn now it pricks my harte
always one sided
      static one wheeled cart
   A rose is my harte
     helpless, closed at night
      When she shines in the sky like moonlight
destined, suffering it can not share her light
       Too rich she is, too trifle is he
       for he fragrance her art
  rose the king of flower, is sought not
    only flower that open in night
  All the world treasures she has
      treasures that world can admire
     my treasures are unseen, in her eyes valueless
      boasting, feel like a liar
My harte aches to for breaking today
     Each petal apart
   make this grey Earth, its grave
     OH! I am not so brave
If after such labours not a harte I command
      a harte that knows me well
   if even it can't bestow a drop of love
      Can't requite for petty reasons
It though I am the only one
    and if I in her eyes am nothing
  if even after such Endeavour
    on such low plane she is living
If even now, security she is hunting
    and if I feel everything
  death again knocks at my door
   as before
  this thorn of love is savagely
    mutilating my harte's core
    is piercing every petal
before in a long list of insane genius

Too deep is my fear of being despised
remember . . . . remember my advice
    I want a hand, casually you don't take
and if you want me, sacrifice I, you make
        or else sacrifice me
            for a secured life
too deep is my blood's hue
        kill from a distance
    your rich clothes it can stain
    a stain too deep
    pain will devour—for you
            too slightly love
    there will be no o'er leap

Sumirasko
259 Dt. 18.01.1993, 9.30 A.M.

My Verses

Have wings not but flies in open space
      have feet not but dances with grace
   run the gauntlet of critics
      my love's relic
Timeless moments trapped in worlds
      trapped words invoking timeless emotion
    sounding deep within
      have vision too keen
    Images amazing, no eyes are seen
    what you feel not
      they just make you feel that
    on right foot you are just caught
Self expression of virtues and vices
      there are different, many devices
    her angelic voice, my verses echo
      as beatific as they the contagion Gecko
The snowy diamond peaks of mountain
    or the green grass, spring fountain
  lover's embrace or masked faces
    honestly potray my verses
churned butter from bittered curd
    from restless pain for many absurd
verses come to life, I hold dearer than mine
      my hart's beat, my harte's pulse
They make me do, all little work I do
      they run as blood in my being
      When ephemerally motion stops, the pen stains
    for hot moment is dead my name
They have eternized me and my love
    have given a new philosia
  they fear neither the critic's stone
        or critic's scissors
    for me they are, not my mirror

Sumirasko
157 Dt. 03.09.1993, 5.00 P.M.

Truly far

Mountains of cloud that hover
      moving mountains in the sky
oh! how they move, some fast, some slow
      Some flying like an arrow
dancing in the cool breeze
      with joy myself is seized
An Eagle flies seems to compete
      Eagle flies seems to enjoy
the contrast of black to white
      a far lovely emotional sight
A mountain I see with yellow peak
      golden colour—pierces deep
tearful clouds freely distributing
      emotions natural
      to a natural man
Potraying strange shapes on heaven's breast
      clouds they just don't rest
until they fall splashing the earth
      laughing as they fall with mirth
a natural man who stares above
      feels the pulse, feels the life throb
The clouds are beatific messengers
      that beauty lies in natural disorder
      Life needs not a formal peace pattern
see how the clouds struggle and run
      lightening is their natural weapon
yet, Amazingly sublime is their war
they are close to nature, we are truly far

Sumirasko
144 Dt. 01.09.1993, 5.40 P.M.

Come on

Come on heavenly love
  in this night like day
a million stars shine
  shine to see you my 'fay'
I will seed a touch
   plant a touchy kiss
the tree of love will grow
  We will rest under its shadow
Come on, come a little more close
  in my love's embrace come my rose
We will feel life, drink from sweet chalice
Will haunt us no more any human malice
Come on 'my love' this is a real moment
   come you need not any artificial ornament
   to reveal your angelic innocence
  is enough my love a sublime askance
come see the spring is here
   see life flows so near
  a drop we both can drink by chance
  feel the flying shallow, grow heavenly wings
   Come share this high romance

Sumirasko
143 Dt. 01.09.1993, 2.30 P.M.

Unseen Love

How much lonely is this day
my hope intoxicated
only upon a hopeless belief
will not wither away any day
the hue of this unseen green love's leaf
In Desperado, in bitter confusion
every real dream seems an illusion
raw passions that only beasts feel
bitter reason mercilessly fights
trapped I am between
my hearts hue is red
not even a tear I can shed
behaving in a manner mawkish
I can become a laughing stock
Will my restraint make you my enemy
Will my disclosure, meets with rejection
I am unsure of either
Cannot behave as the wind behaves
got to have some restraint
crushed in between
my love helpless will
remain unseen

Sumirasko
142 Dt. 01.09.1993, 12.30 P.M.

Tired

Tired I feel, tired at last
the brain seems to be falling
      hands fall at last
The breeze that blows
      is not within my reach
  I want to educate the mortals
      but I could no more preach

Tired I feel, consumed by daily routine
      creator is destroyed, is very lean
thin and pale his face
      the brooks, streams demand rest
tired of this love and hate
      tired of being always precise
      Creating not late

The faulty biological clock is mine
       which pushed me too far
I have reached to the top
      burnt like a star
Like a phoenix I have risen million times
      tired I am, tired at last
Want a peaceful break, an hour peaceful
      the breeze of love, days beautiful

Sumirasko
140 Dt. 31.08.1993, 4.15 P.M.

Little or No

When thought conceals within
a thought
when expressions conceal within
an expression
that cannot be thought
        cannot be expressed
the condition of our soul
        is truly desperate
When our ears hunt for a word
hear thousands but that one eludes
when our eyes search for some expression
find many that one misses
moistens our subjective selves
    a sublime pain, the world seems
      a voracious den
Helpless we are thrown on ocean waves
at the mercy of wind, at the mercy of moon
at the mercy of fate, at the mercy of love
We think, we express, we hear, we see
thoughts thousand, expressions that tortuous
the swelling tide throws us in mid-air
takes a wanton delight in our momentry flight
oh! yet we do look at the world
    for a second from some height

Down again in the Jaws of merciless men
who give again
eternal sorrow—eternal pain
we look for thoughts, expression, words
to soothe the soul
only to find that in destiny outer world
We have little or no role
Can get little or no role
Can get little or no love
Little or no is our eternal fate
for we are born ages before, not late
Little or no, little or no
for us, Pro is contra, contra is Pro
mixed together seeing reality in both
in between we stand
on little or no physical land

Sumirasko
141 Dt. 01.09.1993, 9.30 A.M.

In a dark room

In a dark room my body is camped
eyes see not the hands
yet they move in their locks
desperate, accipitrally insane
Confined in a dark universe
only inky, inky colour
tired at last, my eyes close
not a ray the darkness bestow
My eyes are closed but I see
shadows now—dancing feet
from right they move to left
from left to right
moving shadows, shadows without sight
This is the internal world
that knows not the dark room
is confined not by gloomy gloom
As images appear; faces I do know
talking to me friends and foe
this is the dark inner world
for darkness is light
Not trapped in space, know not fright
as I comeback from an hour
long pilgrimage
haunts me this outer blackness
this unbreakable dark room
suffocating like cage

Sumirasko
139 Dt. 31.08.1993, 4.05 P.M.

Vices Eternized

Your vices I truly praise
        for thou vices are golden
    faults of an innocent rosy spirit
          true subject for limerick
                mostly composed
    I will eternize even them
          with my immaculate pen
       they will shine brighter than all world's virtue
          except for you lovely traits
  When your face potrays death like pale
         in confidence eats your mind
       there can't be a soul in conditions such
        who is more generous, more kind
This only vice I know else
       you have a golden voice
    that surpasses infant smile
       your lies have more truth than truthful lies
you haven't come from heaven's above
         yet you were a spirit once
    your spiritual nature I really praise
       though it is hazy and bare
        is only
All other vices that you may have
       concealed from me, in any form
  rose is neither whole nor beautiful
       unless it has some pricking thorns concealed
  You are a blooming rose my love
       your blooming smile conceals some faults
you are immaculate my friend
       only one in these Earthly lands

Sumirasko
138 Dt. 31.08.1993, 3.45 P.M.

Come into me 'O God'

In books ecstasy I shiver
       shivering joy is mine
   melt into my soul
      make it a shining gold
In these moments I can feel your impalpable touch
      Shimmer my spine with divine love
Come make my part a whole
      come from the basest cores
I think not now just my pen invokes
      Lighten my heavy yoke
this moment, this very moment is mine
      an eternal world before me shines
Death seems a foolish dream
      everywhere is life's eternal stream
my eyes amazed feel the inner world
      the outer seems purposeful-not absurd
There is beauty all around
      for my eyes are divine
Life looks a great musical poetry
      which hath reason and rhyme
I have found my God
      my God I see in me
in angelic beauty happily altruistic
      like the swaying fruit ladden tree

Sumirasko
137 Dt. 31.08.1993, 3.12 P.M.

I must have been like

When I go to bed at four in the morn
       in twilight hours I think this
if I had a previous birth
      I must have been like them
Carefree, worldly, making moves without shame
      I must have been like
a festful boy of wealthy parent
       playing in pounds
       or as an young youth
    flirting with enough girls
         wearing necklaces of real pearls
Doing all that the age demanded
and then one day to marriage remanded
     I must have a heavenly wife
   must have thanked the virtuous life
        had children, nursed them well
and thou when old age approached
          heard the last
     I must have cursed
      'what wasted time'
And then when I died
     they all bid me farewell

Sumirasko
136 Dt. 31.08.1993, 2.37 P.M.

The Blank Paper

Blank faces I meet every day
    Blank soul, not a single ray
Blank steps tread every road
    some high some low
      swerving men faithless men
        feeling less men attacking
        they know not they are just faking
          collecting diamonds which are just stones
    or content in poverty they are just stones
stone men envying, vying one another
        Consumer goods they all are
    durables rusted they all need a repair
      Across the world, throughout the globe
the wind that now blows
    the wind of eternal sorrows
the rich and poor at the mercy of morrow
    lustful life will end is dust
a moment they all must feel
    a moment of inner reality
        they all must
  Then they will know
      everyone of them has a blank paper
    which lies crumbled in dusty
      hartes waste box
unless they justify its worth
    they will know not life and death will full
in grave they will remain
    without a real mark or real name
each one of thee, a blank-blank paper
    with grey dusty Earth for the bores
      a durable eternal wrapper

Sumirasko
135 Dt. 31.08.1993, 2.15 P.M.

Death–The Brute

When grips me the passion of untimely death
unnatural voices speak to me
million faces I have seen
        in so short a life
    million vices I have in me
        my ink is not dried yet
        torments me the horror of an untimely death
When poeply say I am approaching her
        my face is pale, flesh is bone
    smile is a weathered wreath
      for I live alone, alone
oh! the mirror breaks with a mournful cry
    each living truth seems a death like lie
yet, what will happen when I will cease
    locked will be grave forgotten will be keys
will anyone remember these insane days
    or the blackness of night will devour
    each moment of life, my each hour
In youthful slumber when I will die a wreck
    will any one love me for loving's sake
And pay a lamenting tribute
    Such things I think when pen stops
    holds me the horror of death the brute

Sumirasko
133 Dt. 31.08.1993, 11.55 A.M.

She was a fair Sight

She was fair sight
    my bonnie lass, my future bright
on her I leaved
    on her I hoped
When in darkness I groped
    my had in my hands
when touched me . . . teared me
    the hungry lands
She was a beautiful rose
    without thorns
which bloomed everyday
        at night, at morn
When warm breeze touched her
      it used to turn so cool
I watched, I gazed, I stared like a fool
        And still the wind did soothe me
When it touched my soul
     such was the intensity of my feelings
I dreamed of her, watched even
      her apparation
She was a frail sight
     even in her shadow condition
A beautiful strange rose without thorns
    which bloomed every day
        at night, at morn
    She was a fair sight
    made my future look bright

Sumirasko
134 Dt. 31.08.1993, 1.36 P.M.

When Love Calls

Strange passion of a youthful harte
Sun seems to shine in her flesh and blood
the ben of beauty veiled
      is thrilled when love calls
    Her infant smile gives a lesson or two
        which the rose imitates soaked in dew
her fragrance is of rarest species
        the flower ashamed unrolls
    and all is when the love calls
Her face is a cosmic mirror
        yet on Earth she treads is so near
    her hue is of such a golden colour
          snow strives for it all
    and all show up when love calls
When love calls
      the emotions roll
    half breath is her whole life
      a faint voice dictates her strife
as she runs the world stops
        looks with amazed eyes
She disappears in her lover's embrace
When love calls a pretty face

Sumirasko
132 Dt. 31.08.1993, 10.53 A.M.

Dracula

In the woods the owls roost
   on pine trees
   the winter sun lost in mist
   each day is night—grips strange nemesis
The Vampic that sucks blood
   Sensually, Taraquir's ravishing strive
   a living grave for mortals
   his teeth piercing their flesh
   a girl small . . . just now is dead
Her body is a chimney burnt
      black without a drop of blood
   the impaler of the order of dragon
      with beady eyes wake away
   The gale is fast, the trees sway
      it's midnight moon
   the victim is dead
      sparks lit the sky
   the selenian burns in fire
      the thunder breaks and falls
   the Dracula is full of curase
        full of gall
Blood of thousands run in his vein
      unsanctified vices freely reign
Each victim gave him his hue
      he is a stranger, mixture of nature's dew
Ephimeral lives that are alive in him
      make him ghastlier than Gorgon's

Each night when the old clocks strike twelve
the night when full moon dwells
the world is vigilant, nature goes insane
Dracula sensual walks out again
again a murder, his life their grave
fear him cowards
fear more the brave
for vlad Tepes Dracula for them graves

Sumirasko
131 Dt. 31.08.1993, 9.45 A.M.

Wind of Remembrance

Has the wind of remembrance
       ceased to blow
   or it still haunts your harte
       haunts she, my helpless gaze
     gaze of love—gaze of a sage
Do you still remember
      the past that is lost
   dry leaves are dry or are they green
   lying in your love's book unseen
      do you still turn the pages
   or have you burnt the book
        my dove flying in new spaces
          breaking my love's cage
But I still preserve for you
      those ravell'd sleave of care
   those mute hours—thousands of them
     those million askewing stares
I have risen in love through death
      like a pheoenix with eternal health
   static I still feel you are near
     compose verses—completely losing you
               I fear
   you are lost in these forest of walls
      yet secured is your memory 'my love'
  the wind of remembrance is stronger than ever
     if I die again I will die in your love's fever

Sumirasko
130 Dt. 31.08.1993, 8.55 A.M.

Celestis

Not in graves they will go
      not in masses of kites
   they will procure heaven
      soar after death to distant skies
This is a material world
      now they build a material sky
   guranteed existence bodily existence
      for sixty three million years as they say
This is the modern age
    we have now rocketed sages
   living for such infinite time
      salvation within their grasp
          —it's fine
For an Earth we have little space
      little to busy the dead
   We will cremate them not
      until a space ticket is bought
Buy an entrance ticket for heaven
      you need not a God
   fool was Ivan, weak like a karmazov
      who returned, we just now cannot applaud
For Dostoevsky is a distant history
      celestis is a new mystery
   just live somehow in every week of days seven
      procure a ticket reserve a place
          in the seventh heaven

Sumirasko
129 Dt. 31.08.1993, 7.53 A.M.

My Moon

This is a lovely, lovely moon
    ecstasy of my love
black shadow she cares not
    her beauty make me joyfully soaring
near the hill she shines
    so close to Earth she dives
the Earth feasts on her rays
    this night is brighter than days
She passes close to hanging star
    Each star want to touch
be with her as long it can
    begs her rays, in each hand a pen
Innocent she is, she gives to each his due
    and when clouds cover, she veils herself
Let them have her for a minute few
    hangs from her a raindrop, a dew
A drop of love with which
    She quenches my thirst
She is my lovely, lovely moon
    in her embrace I sleep, in her love I swoon

Sumirasko
127 Dt. 30.08.1993, 10.30 A.M.

There was no beauty

There was no beauty on Earth before
now, your weaved voice, like some magical spell
binds me my love the singing wind doth tell
roaring waves take their voice form you
has taken a bit, the cuckoo
Love that seem to swell and sway in them
is all your my love
only echoes in your voice, the dove
They all sing, they all chant words of real praise
to your crystal voice dance sun rays
as capitaved I hear, the music that give
fays hover above showing many a kiss
saying in a voice low
There was no beauty, with this golden voice
in front you they bow
She has given life to clays dead
natural toys
And my believe, my love soars higher in lieu
there was none, there is no one as
beautiful as you

Sumirasko
128 Dt. 30.08.1993, 6.40 P.M.

Confession

I have broken every rib of my body
the twenty four faiths one need to be upright
you all can pull me down, pull down my love
my eyes will still gaze at the heaven above

I am surrounded by sublime frailities
too weak to climb any height
too weak to swim even in shallow sea
helpless the moving fast world I just see

Each shining face, every playful jest
makes me feel a jester
moaning alone in a world stuffed with fest
too gory is the strature rest

And I have not faith, no faith I have
helpless I am no pretensions of being brave
even a butterfly is more for fortunate
She can faith her beatific wings
                    —no one can hate
Insecurity grips me in her cold Iron claws
Security comes for a moment—there are no law
defined to make my life easy
my bravery lies in this
            I confess myself is a sissy

Sumirasko
125 Dt. 30.08.1993, 9.30 A.M.

The Mystery Joyful

When clouds rattle, lightening falls
I am amazed at the magic that unrolls
or when the clear blue sky looks so clear
the sun that shines upon birds I hear
their voices throb with life
suffers gusto serene this world
Each moment the divine is unfurled magic
In the very experience that my heart beats
blood flows, nerves quiver, I walk, I think
there can't be a magic more natural
fools they run after the magic man virtual
Who hovers in mid-air or walks on water
their eyes applaud only his feats
while they see not the greatest magic
that lies near thee they work and eat
What can be a greater romance
a greater learning
then to be amazed at the beatific world
the everlasting harmony that surrounds
if the night ends day is bound
if the spring comes, bees will humm
my eyes now stare at each swaying leaf
there is a magic in each sway
there is a mystery in each speck of dust
each time see and analyse
the mystery deepens, deepens my lust
to know that eludes
the joyful mystery each moment deludes

Sumirasko
124 Dt. 30.08.1993, 9.05 A.M.

Only human

I have scratched your name on the winds
      several times I have played this game
in the darkness of the night, in the ray
      on dark winds on dark day
            like this today
This morn looks as distressed as me
            her face as pale
      the stillness is an uneasy calm
            before the storm the fast gale
Dark clouds echo, this portrayal is mine
            nature paints herself today
      in my immaculate style
            show of desperation, simple without quite
Your name I inhale, try to lean upon a void
the moment next the wind oh! she gets annoyed
the breath goes, too angelic is your innocence
      Cannot with hold for than a moment
            I have no patience
I scratch again thou name, again in hale
            rest with it for a moment then turn pale
            your name is so divine I shiver when I speak
      the vibrations in the void make me weak
I move, I swerve, I break, I frail
this black morn, potrays my love's gall
Come my love before I scratch again
Come like a wind, fill my harte 'O' fair
      surround me in a blanket of love and care
falsify this black morn's potrayal
      be a little less angelic 'O fay'
      I am only human

Sumirasko
124 Dt. 30.08.1993, 9.05 A.M.

The Stare

Helpless as a child he sat
a clawless hare
feeling a very fuming breath
trapped in a snare
No means to escape the torment
its were not there
to Samaritan gruesom third degree subjected
Can any one call it fair?
he felt morally weak like a thief
like a thief punished for felony
and the air that throbbed with death
spoke tender words of irony
A sudden movement, a search light
ahoe that at last the saviour was in
with holding breath, he breathed not
the poisioned air, waiting for the fresher
            when she was in
Moments doubtful, hell for a waiting harte
with each tread the Earth shook twice
when it came near, grew double his fear
Listened hard with triple ear

A shadow he saw, convinced was he
at last she came—it was she
ten paces ahead—'O' Dear
he recognised not herself—gripped again the fear

The way she was dressed it was
lovely and queer
the faces seemed strange
he understood not the meaning of her stare

The stare that shocked and confused
Was it someone else he mused
What hell! what crude hell
Whose stare was it, he couldn't tell
Too Vunerable a tortoise without his shell
in complete insecurity he swooned, he fell

Sumirasko
123 Dt. 30.08.1993, 7.25 P.M.

Real Roses

I present you with blooming roses
  blooming roses in my silly dreams
And hope you will reply
  reply in the day light scene
Do you feel love—my heavenly friend
  feel love in my dream
  feel the touch of my crude hand
  I just make such castles of sand
They break my harte breaks
  When I see the waking weather
  a dove escaping my sight
  not knew flying thither
In these real Earthly rays
  I always ask what next?
  the dove can never go so deep in haste
  her flight real is just best
If I could be like you 'my love'
  just on the surface like that dove
  on the surface hovering like a butterfly
  If I could with myself lie
If I could convince myself 'all is well'
  see the world through a worms eye cry hail!
and just believe in some power
  so very happy will be your lover'
Thou I can reveal make all wordly moves
  in a common world a common man
will you then be proud of me
  if I present you real roses which you can see
If I knew you, just a little not much
  if I care in a carefree manner
will you find me easy, if I tie not a deep knot
  present you real roses for shallow love show bought

Sumirasko
121 Dt. 29.08.1993, 3.25 P.M.

On College

College they say is the door to wisdom
'poor souls' swooping each hear at each lecture
     bits of broken pottery, never whole
       of different ages and time
   running helter skelter at each call
         at each chime
    Its chemistry, history, Mathematics and Physics
    they learn nothing other than poorest limerik
    Poor souls 'repeating each day and day'
    will they ever see the hey day
The pierian spring, the exploring mind
is reduced to hollow degrees in this
          mill of time
In the same degree block each sprinter is
   Some fast—some slow for degree run
this is a college of sprint this
    not of genuine original concerns
And what of most professors that teach
    the subject is beyond their reach
   just blind imitation, parroted diction
    words from their mouth escape
  escape like facts in mid-air turn fiction

The college is a gruesome call of this age
where they devour the past burn every future page
where they step in just for a future easy
gulp every medicine down, to look like a healthy
Tread miles to keep themselves fit
yes, college is wisdom, feels the walls well lit
but wisdom really is theirs
      who chose to opt
   enjoy the freedom in learning out of it street
      enjoy their original nature
for college is for those paralysed
    who need a crutch
are running desperately degrees as such

Sumirasko
89 Dt. 24.08.1993, 12.00 A.M.

The Magic Morphia

Like a swallow if you have lost
          your mark in the slumber hours
     morning across the waste lands
           sure to land in a morass
or if thou are a timoneer lost
         without oars in the tempest
     or the rut—affairs have become boring
          you want a chance—for perfect scoring
come with me to the magic room
         take this magic morphia
   And thou will feel, the elating mood
          will spirit away any meloncholia
He be phorenic acts, demand explanation
        this feeling is self exploration
   no foolish bargain dare you call
        bare—footed walk, in sky stroll

II

Here now, feel yourself
        the ringlet ring steady or blowing
   close your eyes, black image appears
      close and outer world disappears
Arouse your will, to a new imagination
       in mind's sky a window filled
    build it up—you are the creator
      stuff you have—you are the oracle

III

This a different world
    from whence you came through the slit
  Here are blue mountains
     towering high
blue water runs—there is a stream
  you are conscious unlike a dream
and swallow that fly in the sweet sun
love is here in abundance
    in each and every one
And if you decide to live here
    not go back to the waste lands
the magic morphia will surely heal
    your body will be in the grave
      dug up by your friends

IV

You have found a world so beautiful
    no amount of gold can buy
and if some sceptics doubt
    let them once try
They will never come back, I assure you
   to pronounce magic morphia is a lie

Sumirasko

The Wounded Man

Like a flush, it's all same
      throughout the body
  of the same intensity
    of same inflammation
the prior has gnashes
     they say it's a pretending game
has a half broken white cup in front
    has no legs, has no arms
  and they say, 'it's just a stunt'
Below a tree, amidst plenty foliage
    the wounded man sits
no fomentation, only wet rain
    West breeze—wastes away
    the trail sane
A painter potrays, a poet versifies
    he sits therefore ordained
to become a subject of brush and pen
    'Why don't me they slain'
And of mental agony, his face speaks
     eyes sunken in, he has little nose
   seems to say but keeps mute
    the world passes day by day
     the day pass
  the tree remains, the wounds remain
yellow stream flows in rain
    and red blood that is mixed
  keeps the wound green
    such green leaves of tree
below which the man sits
    in all the world you will never see an imagery
    he is an wounded man for a poet just

Sumirasko
84 Dt. 23.08.1993, 6.30 P.M.

Lost in the wild

He says 'he lost her in the wild'
    adds 'she was self–styled'
    but no one knows where the woods were
    what beasts now take her care

He says 'he too is lost'
    adds 'the future is past'
    but no one knows what present is
    on what turns, he accepted pain's loose

And he say 'the pain is incurable'
    adds 'sweet is sour'
but no one knows if he ever tasted sweet
well how he knows sweet exists

And he may then quote every great man
    and prove that he is a suffering insane
    But well that is the way the world is
    send him to an asylum, he will know
    the loss of freedom is worse
    than losing on self in the wild

Sumirasko
68 Dt. 22.08.1993, 11.02 A.M.

More than Mother

In the vortices of life's river
there is depth too much
you escape one, the second lies at hand
you escape the second, the third waits
  until all fall in the losts in oceans depth
    some earlier, some late
      drowned is their fate
Each whirlpool cries into you
    'come measure my depth'
  you escape like owls of day
    yet, to the last all fell an easy prey
That wipes you such
    you forget yourself
  your vox is lost forever
    security there is none
  in the jaws of death, no shelter
There is no eden, no heaven
  only fire burns in the hell seventh
  you escape one, the second waits
  until forced you fall in the last
    verily late
And easy stream can give clayey leisure
but in depths, in vortices lies real treasure
see every vortex cries
    come measure my depth
Put up a brave front, leave the raft
  fall heading in melancholia
  better today than tomorrow
    with your own will not for code
  fed the deepest sorrow
    the darkest breeze that blows inside
  great tantrums that rage
    will bring down you image sage

In the Black light you will feel
    you can devour deaths darkness at will
And then will, you will rise to face another
When the lightening last strikes
you will know yourself more
    than you will know your mother

Sumirasko
72 Dt. 23.08.1993, 4.25 P.M.

In a Saloon

(After visiting a saloon)
Dumb sitted in a saloon
 feeling the atmosphere strange
 hairs that coil even in faronian wind
 how neat hands arrange
A child of fair complexion
 a smaller to describe
one can not find a lexicon
 can say he was black
 can say he was poor
 can say he was hesitating
too found the barber's machine
 after the ceromonial throning
Every one payed to be a king
 his orders were restricted
 to moustaches and hairs
 everyone sat on elevated chairs
A man with a paper
 read spiritualism
 how the highest contemplation
 can raise his ism's
And the child dozed off
 the man with the scissor
answered his sublime movements
 with an innate acumen
that surpassed all poetic merchants
And there was superstition
 for counting bad omen a green pepper
 and for good a money-plant creeper
 forever in demand
 and if some one did pay a tip
 a blooming smile returned his gift
 and idle talk was a currency hot
 for persons of a general sort

The saloon was a royal palace
    where a man was groomed
        to king's grace
  for a few bucks, the power was yours
      in a saloon, the wizard men plays host
      your spirit rise
        a new look boast
    and if you were a satanic at heart
          you can walk out 'O' Saint
        make a new start

Sumirasko
69 Dt. 23.08.1993, 6.50 A.M.

La Dien de La Danse

(Nijinsky)
Dedicated to Vaslav Nijinsky

Nijinsky was his name
    people allege in late life he went insane
        who was responsible?
           the world binded him in chains

I

Come back time or take me back
in the golden days
      When this sage lived
  or confer prophetic eyes
        to rediscover his heart grieved

II

Here I see him in the Imperial School of dancing
        He is alone meditating
    upon his rotating feet
      the Earth small seems imitating
  His eyes closed penetrate
          deep down
  he is in an inward man
      living in himself
  always in touch while in motion
    with his deepest self
The breeze is his name in petersburg
and sings to his dance every lark
He plays the Petrushka, he is a Petrushka
He plays the hunchback, he is a hunchback
  dismisses his identity at will
he is La Dien de La Danse Nijinsky
    elating or bringing his personality to Nill

He is a living Buddha
        not a Buddha in making
   a radiating face—bright halo
        a body more than mellow

He is innocent
        here I see he pays the price
   is seduced by Diaghileff
upon the conditions advise

His brother is mentally retarded
        his father deserted his mother
   and here so penurious helpless
        he is La Dien de La Danse awarded

III

Motion is his forte
        in motion he feels at home
   Cries 'I am God, I am God'
        such is his realization strong
And here he escapes the bends
        loves and marries a hungarian
   like him a dancer, a samaratian
   Establishes theatre—he is blundering
        for he is a inward man—inept
                at arranging
        the work is angular in his hands
   a spiritual force building dunes of sand
He suffers and here starts the first war
        his face is full of scares
   full of human love, full of prophetic altruism
        he human triviality human weakness
             war sadism

His diary is full of bloody red lines
        strange statements
   and I can see the desperation in his eyes
        the malebolge torments

Here is standing an a village street
with his cross outside asking too keen
      Every passer by 'Have you gone to the church
      And they all leave him in the lurch
His wife as informed, Nietzsche did the same
      a sort while after he is pronounced insane
      He is for ably, taken to one asylum

IV

Too supersensitive he never came out
      dwelled deeper down
nothing lured him back
      not even his unchallenged
I see he died in a twilight zone
      from world completely at lorn

V

'The life of my wife and all mankind is death' said he
      in death he is now alive
      dancing still to the cosmic strife
He who declared 'I am God'
      was a true bayard
      And the word dead, as a tribute
      which places the ceremonial wreath
Falsely proclaims la Dien de La Dance
      Vaslav Nijinsky is dead

Sumirasko
71 Dt. 23.08.1993, 11.25 A.M.

Always Near

I sleep with your dreams
      on my hands are your lines
   in my eyes your face
        the sweet breeze that kisses my body
      takes all . . . . . . all my stress
Like a sweet self you came to me
       in thee is a sublime tender
   that surpasses the tenderest flowers
       is above the greatest wonder
   such is the sweetness of your homely love
And then for a moment, when you escape
      I am alone with beatific landscape
   with their dynamic intensity
     you come back
   and my stare a wild gape
when my eyes slowly open like a flower
     after a night long slumber
   your face still is near, soaked in may–dew
     not dissolved in saline tears
   your lines are on my hand still 'O Dear'

Sumirasko
Dt. 22.08.1993, 10.45 A.M.

Back and fill Life

He sits on an anxious seat
  accused of idolatory
 fiasco is a stop away
   flippont is not he
 harcking back to post 'his prithee'
The weather too over him is inclement
  the head over the shoulder is a torment
 and hey–day just come and go
  in between darkness rules his kingdom
Zillion curses tell his nerves
  he knows not the esperante of love
In a moment, the world is a million suns
   all burning bright
 the next not a hand is chanced
  in noon–day light
He cares for persons too much
  knows not they forget history
 loves and lacerates himself so much
   To back and fill his life

Sumirasko
64 Dt. 22.08.1993, 7.45 A.M.

Just Now

How lonely were the roads
on which I walked till now
Just and now I make the same mistakes again
in my share why falls only pain, eternal pain

Just now my whole body is warm
and ears bums out of shame
An undisclosed fear beats my harte
and blood that flows poisons my eyes

Just now I hear western music
now my spine shivers—I feel weak
my eyes are drowsy I can't see
all is gloom, all is desperation

Just now a black bed eats me up
fed up with life—I seek death
But even death fears my feeling
so deep a blackness even it can't take

Just now I don't know any body else
no ambition can just now wake me
only me is here, this is my ambit
here is the nose–dive I am always worried
Just now the feeling is love, is luxury
there is no good time in my dictionary
I will see my wet moon some night?
even this lure, gives a fright

Sumirasko
64 Dt. 22.08.1993, 7.45 A.M.

On Critics

They say as the word goes
they would stop at each take a pause
And central you poets
      control your harte thumping wild
    for here comes the critic
      with a scissors self–styled

He weighs each one of them
      on a crude balance pan
    and then passes a judgement
      'compared to classics insane'
And he is a critic of modern art

What labour pains you faced for this creation
      he will see in it nothing but vaulting ambition
    he will raise his pen—a six thousand feet high wall
      will try his best that you don't check your fall

In a vehmant mood they still say
    we spared not Dickens
and compared you are mere chicken
    but from whence you came
      to disturb our peaceful slumber
which we graved all cocks and hens

So beware of critics before you dip, ink the pen
    put a brave esteemed front
criticize yourself before they compare you with
    all their dead cocks and hens

Sumirasko
65 Dt. 22.08.1993, 8.30 A.M.

In the Present Sky

What glowly gloom? presumed dead
like from heavens a star single shed
that falls not straight, in a curved trajectory
near the Earth extinguish its battery
And those few, which hit, leave a crator
in the crator you can find the alligator
that haunts you all life long
         for they leave a mark too strong
Not erased from all world's memory
         they live not die in the grave's dormitory
    And you foolish dreamers
              emulate them—to become them
and forget your path unique
              which is your own chaletry
Erase the dead, awake from dream
              I command thee
         to face the challenge
                   in a manner keen
shine like a star in the present sky
         do not become a victim of Earths predator
get inspiration from your own light
         dependence on past is a mere fright
A mere flight from you own potential
    I tell thee to find the rational
and if thou find you are alive in breath
    thou shine, light your path not
                        worry for the dead

Sumirasko
66 Dt. 22.08.1993, 9.45 A.M.

The Secret Lover

What great eyes thou have?
what greater thou life lips!
all my prayers starts with you
for all my secrets thou keep
What inquisitiveness thou show!
what gentleness thou bestow
all my manners have changed with you
this change is a thing rare and new
And when thou read my thoughts in a pause
I fumble desperately to add a chance
what great patience thou have a 'doll'
always waiting not forcing me to the wall
What name thou can give?
no name can do justice, every one will be a lie
yet, when the breeze blows I call you so
like when the wet moon shines, I see you so
These are things not which can thou believe
those one things internal, not on my face
                              thou can see
And so let these thing remain a secret
for even of thou say 'I care' thou can
                    morrow easily reject

Sumirasko
62 Dt. 21.08.1993, 1.20-1.35 P.M.

The Mud

Call all the heavens, call every beast and bird
        here lies a dog mouthing blood in Mud
see his eyes closed are smeared
        here goes a sophisticated girl
    here I see–she falls like a bird
She is dead they say,
        She saw hell before she died
And now they say 'she would go straight'
        but for now in mud her today lies
some one tries to revive
        Mud is body, soul is life
    Complacent thinkers soothing their mind
        they carry their soothing their mind
        repeat at intervals 'I am alive'
only on this internal conservation
        they base their life
And whenever a relative is mud
        Alas! they fear every dead bird
only a magical spell,
        keeps the mud monument
Somehow upright
        once you meditate, you
    know mud is trifle for mundane life
        is the best means for cosmic strife
    for in the very body mud secret lies
        unravelling the secret givers it a meaning

Sumirasko
61 Dt. 21.08.1993, 12.40 A.M.

At Dawn

Night by clock has eloped with stars and heaven
                it's dawn, forced retirement
            darkness had shed tears
                        upon the glass blades its dew
        in the air mist and fog
                    the sun fights a gruesome battle
            against night left overs
Earth shimmers, shivers in the cold
                dismal surrounding
        which the lover scold
                Not a hand is seen
        to work, not a child is at play
                this dawn is going too
                    be a moony day
And hear what the flowers say
                it's too cold out here O 'Sun' wept
            arrest this cold out here O 'Sun' wept
        And hear what the stream say
            we fail our path, please answer soon
            give our life a new lease
                            a new moon
And they wait today in vain
            for the sun only fights a showy battle
        has no mettle, has a grain of shame
                will never come out again
For it has killed the heavenly moon
                now the night mourns over this ruin

Sumirasko
58 Dt. 21.08.1993, 6.30 A.M.

Now its my Turn

'O' my undisclosed friend
      you have potrayed me in differin shades
  now its my turn
      come to the ground hear the truth bare laid
What thou eyes saw in me
      never I knew for sure
   yet I knew for all my speculation
      there was some gruesome desperation
Not a word direct came to me
   only songs at a high pitch kept pouring
And they too had different shades
   never I knew for sure of what clay thou are made
And when we used to meet in streets
    you avoided always a gaze
What could I infer
    I was in a maze

you never wrote me a word
   you never were of the herd
  a strong fear always gripped my nerve—static
    what crazy man of music
And then we were about to depart
   you just stared aghast
you were burning in those moments
you were burning in those moments
  but you never made a move to stop the torment

It was a day you will always curse
    in isolation you will call me still a traitor
  But hear me it the day passed—
      you could not have been much better
  For seven years now from morn to night
        you could leave just liked me alright
    And thou when all was lost
      you had to freeze in the wedding front
  And even then you ran in the night fog
     I saw you wading in sweat
    and my heart doubled 'Dear'
      but you never came to me for fear
of rejection that is a sublime hell
      more better than in which you today dwell
    for the wind in it is taken out of sails
      but you are now riding on ocean waves
And you can potray me still
    in a deity or demon shade
  you lost me then, only this
      much can be the best to feast
    I will win too, if yours is the final conquest

Sumirasko
60 Dt. 21.08.1993, 12.20 A.M.

'Greater than Life'

The shadow has left my side
    the sky black seems so near
  seems to fall the inky sky
    the Earth shimmers seems to cry

This is the fiery past
    burning pages of history
  the fire is blue that turns my clock
    strangely there is no smoke
'O God' there is enough love one here
    but where I hope—it isn't there
metres are lost, the beloved sneaks in
    in verses I everyday paint the heart paining
It's too strange a distance, more than patience
      the breeze that flows tells me
        the black night persists
      I am enclosed in its vicious blanket
    There are no stars here
        stars are not here
    only riddle dreams
      that force mute screams
The shadow never comes back
    the eyes only fume
  there is no crutch to hold, there is no knife
    this night is greater than life
once can escape the whole world
    one can severe any relation
  but tell me 'O' God
    how can one escape self laceration

Sumirasko
57 Dt. 20.08.1993, 6.00 P.M.

The Questioner (Weathered) Leaf

When Earth bears heavens cross upon herself
When darkness encloses her lovely face
he sits alone near a strawful nest
mourning, feeling her cross upon his chest

He remembers the past, each lovely day
forgets not the golden moments nay
And his heart begins to ooze
his hands shiver, firmness loose

He coins new phrases, in this tormented hell
thinks he hears a faint rebel yell
washes his hand in stream
sees the water is stagnant and stale

Resting swallow at peace make him feel
he is stranger, who has lost life's deal
How they sleep in abundance, carefree
and like them must have been sleeping his prithee

And here he is vexed for he thinks too much
Cries life is a search, is a search
but the blowing leaf, withered questions
What he is searching? What is its destination?

Sumirasko
58 Dt. 21.08.1993, 7.05 A.M.

Levin

When those armed dark clouds
        look upon bride's face
     see the greenness, her love's grace
       their eyes wide amazed
   quarrel with each other for fall in
          discharging Levin
Innocent lightening that shrinks
        many a lovers' harte
   falls on a sparrow midway
       burns a castle, burns a dove
  And all because clouds clammer for their love
This is an everlasting troy
       as the fable goes
   when levin falls upon a trifle thing
     it is pure gold and no alloy
     And after claps that are often heard
      are light match his that slowly catch
   When their axe falls there is no match
The world mourns deeply
      when levin charms a human
  but levin is indifferent
    is not disastrous if they have the acumen
And when clouds signalling their beloved
     come falling down
  she embraces them, spreads them
      on her bossom
        or let's them deep down
  Levin is the luxury
     few can watch with glee
yet nothing is human fear
    where nature is to spring
Levin to book anyone can't bring

Sumirasko
56 Dt. 20.08.1993, 4.55 P.M.

India

The spirit this soul spirits away
    slowly dying—the process to final decay
    in making
    is a computed logarithm of centuries
    yet there is hope, there is an optism
The hope is a mirage
         the optimism crutch of mind
    looking for contentment
         glory of past is a gruesome father
       Superstition is alive—man is matter
In this land of poverty
         in the moment one rests on past
    to garb oft the shameful nakidity
         the country shines like a diamond
       but deep below large heaps of coal burn
       stuck in the past
       anything new one doesn't learn
Philosophy of life is not a subject to intuit
    the final word has been passed
         Life itself has become destitute
The treasure every one still has
       the blood that flows in every vein
India itself out of fear stagnant
    the royal life some persues goes in vain

II

The crutch of past must be broken
      faith must precede doubt
    doubting men, doubting the first principle
      in a vehemence strife
  find out for themselves that now is life?
And if they find, Life is as the materialist's say
      let them live up to its merit
    And if they find, Life is spirit
      let them live up to its merit
    But first let them such doubting choice
      and then pass their supreme voice
only then the ancient spirit will revive or disappear
and then I tell thee it will again appear
Today people sleep, let them doubt sleep
      be awake
And then search themselves for truth's sake

Sumirasko
86 Dt. 24.08.1993, 10.10 A.M.

An Insane Walk

Mad tread in a stuffed town
    9.00 a.m. at morn
meandering streets broken
    upon which I walked shaken
thinking and thinking
    Walking and thinking
dragging myself and feeling
    the loneliness in a crowd
Men going to work
    shopkeepers selling goods
boys with their heavy loads
    and girls I followed
A not so virtuous act
    but I fell—nothing I saw nothing
moulds of flesh around me
    my trousers were stinking
the shirt had a button less
    Lost in my own world in a mass
thinking over something
and that something is shivering
    shivering is feeling
in a pot hole
    many are open in my town

And when walks insanely
     above . . . he is very verily prove
so here I am at last home
     sweating, thirsty as before
Neither head nor tails could I make
     Alas! I just want to cry
what's going on?
inside my head, in the world
     And between the two
So confusing is the relation
     I fant in frustration
aye! Insane walk make me frail
And here all laugh in joy
     all enjoy—drink the ale

Sumirasko
463 Dt. 13.10.1993, 11.55 A.M.

An elegy for doomed youth

Why you died so early 'O youth'
　　　why upon the funeral pile 'O young'
why you feel not the cool breeze
　　　why a wonder song, you not sing
why your spirits left so early
　　　evicted a house new
why your name know few
　　　　Alas! no none
you too were born if only to die
at such a tender age
then one may question life?
A straight bullet pierced your heart
　　　　you succumbed then and there
your flesh floating in blood ocean
　　　which you could never swim
　　　　the spirit at once flee away
for some new house I presume
O youth yet this blood is all wasted
　　　　this flesh is of no use
one cannot even eat
　　　　ah! vultures or fire's upon it feast
　　　And the funeral pyres burn 'O youth'
　　　　who killed you?
　　　It was by chance or some feud
　　　　　or romance
　　I know—but blind the oak
　　　　tree—I see a maiden weeping
perhaps in her breast a little secret keeping
　　　a little milk of love
for her doomed lover
　　　O doomed youth
you lost all but these tears
　　　to ablute your sins—if any
　　　a misdemeanor or a felony

Sumirasko
462 Dt. 12.10.1993, 6.50 P.M.